Country Living

RUSTIC HOMES

HEARSTBOOKS

An Imprint of Sterling Publishing Co., Inc.
1166 Avenue of the Americas
New York, NY 10036

ISBN 978-1-61837-177-5

Distributed in Canada by
Sterling Publishing c/o Canadian Manda Group,
664 Annette Street
Toronto, Ontario, Canada M6S 2C8

For information about custom editions, special sales, and premium
and corporate purchases, please contact
Sterling Special Sales at 800-805-5489
or specialsales@sterlingpublishing.com.

Manufactured in China

2 4 6 8 10 9 7 5 3

www.sterlingpublishing.com

Design by Susan Uedelhofen

CountryLiving

RUSTIC HOMES

BARNS, CABINS, COTTAGES & FARMHOUSES

HEARST
books

The porch of this new log cabin in Georgia has railings made from tobacco barn poles.

INTRODUCTION

Here at *Country Living*, rustic abodes are our stock in trade. Virtually not an issue goes by without at least one of these treasures from the past—a farmhouse, cabin, or barn-turned-home—presented in all its glory. And that's not surprising. Whether we live in an antique or a big city high-rise, most of us somehow can't help being drawn to structures that remind us of our history. These rough-hewn buildings harken back to a time when people made their living from the land (either as farmers, ranchers, hunters, or fishermen). Life was far from easy, but people knew the satisfaction of hard work well done. Hours passed more slowly, with time for family and friends, home-cooked meals, and community gatherings. The buildings where people lived and worked still speak of authenticity, of ingenuity—a use-what-you-have ethic—and of a synchronicity with nature rare in modern life. No wonder so many of us fantasize about setting up housekeeping in a charming farmhouse, a cozy cabin, or a weathered barn!

Even if your house didn't start out as such a structure, incorporating the rustic touches they inspire can make modern homes feel warmer, lived-in, and snug. And if you are lucky enough to call one of these buildings home, decorating a truly unique space filled with all kinds of original details is pure pleasure. On the pages that follow, you'll find an abundance of inspiring ideas and gorgeous photographs to help you reclaim, repurpose, refurbish, or restore your way to the country home of your dreams.

CHAPTER 1

CLASSIC DOWN-HOME CHARM

Farmhouses were made for the kind of old-fashioned décor that has delivered tried-and-true country comfort for decades. Quilts on the bed, patterned wallpaper, a chintz-covered chair in the living room—these signs instantly convey that in this house, rough edges are softened with homespun care. Proudly displayed collections of yellowware or jadeite, and treasured antiques such as spindle beds or pine tables, are other hallmarks of a style that says "you've come home."

FARM FRESH
A headboard made from reclaimed shipping pallets with barn lighting gets warmed up with a mohair throw and graphic pillows.

Pattern Play

Fortune favors the bold—it's as true in decorating as anything else. An expanse of wildly patterned wallpaper or a rug pulls a room together and makes an unforgettable statement, all at the same time. Farmhouse style needn't be timid!

Wallpaper inspired by 18th-century botanical prints infuses this snug bedroom with cheerful color and design in keeping with styles and motifs that were popular when the Upstate New York house was built. A pair of vintage iron twin beds and a painted spindle-leg table open up the space.

The formality of the patterned rug is relaxed by a muslin-upholstered couch with linen seat covers, and beautiful mossy green bookshelves and window frames.

Check It Out

Vivid buffalo check fabrics are farmhouse icons and liven up any room. As a bonus, they play nicely with other patterns, such as a multi-colored flowered chintz (opposite page) or lovely floral sheets (below).

Wallpaper with a wood-grained pattern—a fresh way to achieve an effect similar to unpainted, wood-paneled walls—creates a warm backdrop for a standout white-painted bed upholstered with blue-and-white check fabric.

→This spacious family room can easily host a crowd. A streamlined steel-framed coffee table and graphic longhorn watercolor add non-traditional notes to the classic checks and chintz upholstery.

6

BUFFALO CHECKS

IN THE 1850s, PENNSYLVANIA'S WOOLRICH WOOLEN MILLS, THE OLDEST CONTINUOUSLY OPERATING WOOLEN MILL IN THE U.S., INTRODUCED A NEW SHIRT THAT FEATURED WHAT WOULD BECOME ITS SIGNATURE PATTERN: THE BUFFALO CHECK. (RUMOR HAS IT THAT THE WOOLRICH DESIGNER WHO CREATED THE SHIRT OWNED A HERD OF BUFFALO, HENCE THE NAME.) THOUGH RED AND BLACK IS THE ORIGINAL COLOR COMBINATION, THE TERM "BUFFALO CHECK" NOW APPLIES TO ANY FABRIC WITH OVERSIZE SQUARES, WHETHER USED IN CLOTHING OR HOME DESIGN.

Very clever: extra-long curtains perform double duty as a canopy when they're hung from a bed crown instead of a rod.

Sweet Dreams

Cozy inns and B&B's have farmhouses to thank for the distinctive beds—and bedding—that guests find irresistible. Antique styles, creative canopies, and pretty patterned coverlets create beds that make you wish it was time to turn in!

A classic spindle-style pine bed is dressed up with a paisley-inspired coverlet. Warmth is added by a braided rug, and quirky curtains contribute a hint of edge.

A show-stopping antique lighting fixture tops off this airy bedroom. Store-bought sheer panels let in light but maintain privacy. On the bed: a blue block-print quilt.

Understated yet impossible-to-miss wallpaper provides the perfect backdrop for an Empire sofa (updated with mauve velvet) and a large secretary.

An Air of Refinement

Farmhouse style can take a formal bent. Sophisticated wall treatments and European-style antiques create an environment where crystal decanters, silver vases, and equestrian touches are right at home.

The floral flourishes in this dining room look like wallpaper but are actually paper cutouts pasted directly onto the painted walls. A horse portrait on the silver- and crystal-bedecked bar hints at a thoroughbred past.

Art Smart

If you didn't inherit a treasure trove of ancestral portraits or oil paintings, not to worry. Thrift-store finds—even old paint-by-numbers work—can provide artistic interest on the walls, and are proof that sometimes more is more. Up the impact by hanging paintings in groups organized around a theme.

The owners of this home have a rule: the landscape paintings they collect must cost under $100 and include a house. Here, their finds share the stage with a stuffed pheasant perched on the newel post.

A group of botanical paintings adds color and charm to an otherwise neutral parlor. The vintage camp sign was snatched up at a *Country Living* Fair for $50.

WELCOME
VISITORS
PLEASE
REGISTER
HERE

Collected Wisdom

The thrill of the hunt is equaled only by the pleasure of finding creative ways to display and enjoy your bounty every day.

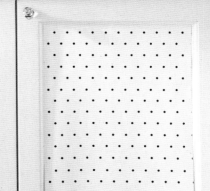

Green glass jadeite pieces are perfectly set off by a white cupboard.

←Wicker picnic and fishing baskets transform mudroom chaos into calm. On the floor, a baguette basket is the perfect height for storing umbrellas.

A coatrack becomes a creative composition of safari hats and photographs—with a little iron Scottie dog for good measure.

Birds of a Feather

You only need a few of a kind to make a statement in a hallway, on a tabletop, or in a kitchen corner.

↑ Colorful ceramic candlesticks reminiscent of antique spindle furniture enliven a dining room table during off-hours.

Displayed on an antique pie safe, a collection of yellowware holds fresh produce as well as antlers found on this Upstate New York property.

Big Personality

Color-saturated walls make a strong statement and work particularly well in small rooms, where the color plays up the space's snug dimensions. Think powder rooms, libraries, or studies, and smaller guest bedrooms like this one.

A four-poster spindle bed outfitted with a striped wool blanket and wood-grain patterned bedding creates a comfy room-within-a-room feel, while botanical curtains add softness and privacy.

A brass lighting fixture that will develop patina over time hangs above a farm table that doubles as an island.

BREAD

Kitchen Magic

Country kitchens aren't always white. The owner of this 105-year-old Texas farmhouse covered the existing white cabinets and beige walls with black paint for a seamless look with surprising warmth.

→ Black beadboard is an excellent backdrop for open shelving displaying the homeowner's collection of antique pewter and a favorite needlepoint ("Kissin' Wears Out: Cookin' Don't").

Red Alert

This intense shade packs a
punch, whether in great swaths
or a patchwork mash-up.

↑ A colorful
old quilt is
repurposed to
upholster a worn
chair. Strips of
brilliant red pull it
all together.

In an Upstate
New York home
where winter
lasts five months
a year, cozy red
walls are the
perfect shade.

→ A mudroom's
brick-red paint
shows off the
clean curves of a
bench found at an
antiques mall in
Great Barrington,
Massachusetts.

BRIGHT IDEA: Branches sliced down on one side (so they'll lie flat) and nailed onto the wall make hooks with rustic appeal.

23

Patchwork-inspired throw pillows add a country welcome to this cheery foyer.

Classic Quilts

Absolutely nothing says farmhouse like a quilt. These handmade heirlooms run the gamut from breathtakingly beautiful to simple, practical patchworks, but all are covetable, collectible reminders of the past.

An antique quilt coverlet with bow and floral motifs gets an update with a traditional country bed frame painted a bright shade of green.

Homespun

Classic country style means using what you've got. Paint doesn't have to be perfect—and it doesn't have to be there at all. Well-worn wood is appreciated for its beauty and utility, and ingenious, one-of-a-kind space-saving solutions only add to the quirky charm.

BRIGHT IDEA: Slots carved into the end of the table store the homeowner's wooden spoons.

A backless bench can be tucked under the farm table when not in use, creating extra space.

Two narrow shelves and a pink(!) marble-topped buffet serve as a coffee station in an otherwise unused corner of the kitchen.

Burlap curtains stylishly conceal utilitarian pots and pans. Equally important, they make room for a console-turned-island that swinging cabinet doors wouldn't have allowed.

Lighten Up

White paint unifies rustic wooden walls and imbues a small house with a sense of spaciousness. The clean, calm look works especially well in bedrooms and baths.

← The bathroom's pitched ceilings made a standard-height shower a no go. Enter a deep, cast-iron soaking tub, purchased for only $100 at a junkyard and then refinished. A yard of cheesecloth hung from Shaker pegs above the window adds a feminine finish that complements the tub.

← A green chalkboard has been hung in place of a headboard, and a floral coverlet adds just enough pattern to keep the room from feeling lifeless.

↓ In this white aerie, a blue cast-iron bed is tucked in front of two windows, enhancing the cozy factor without blocking light.

BRIGHT IDEA: An inconveniently placed support beam is pressed into service as a visual divider for the room.

Bonne Nuit

White Out

For the owner of this 1890s California farmhouse, decorating with white was a practical choice. She saved money by slipcovering furniture she already owned, and white was the perfect backdrop for displaying her beloved quirky vintage finds.

←To create a dining nook, a pine pedestal table and slipcovered armchairs pull up to built-in benches. An ironstone jug holds a mix of hydrangeas and lilacs.

→The living room's bookcases house treasured objects, including bits of architectural salvage, flea-market figurines, and a mid-century clock. A slipcovered armchair is accessorized with a pillow that references the natural world just beyond the walls.

Serene Scene

The loft bedroom in this farmhouse offers guests a lovely retreat in keeping with the homeowners' whole reason for buying a country house: having a place where they "could just be."

BRIGHT IDEA: Fern fronds offer an elegant, easy alternative to flower arrangement.

Lime-green bedding and a new skylight brighten up this space, where a Shaker-style bed by Ikea and a metal side table mingle with an antique desk and bench.

Nicely Neutral

An absence of color can bring polish to a rustic space and seems perfectly at home in a more refined residence.

←Vintage finds bring character to this kitchen: a pine farm table, metal bistro chairs, and a painted hutch that proudly displays the homeowners' collection of milk-glass dishware.

→In this former barn in the Texas Hill Country, white brightens up the rough-hewn floors and unfinished wooden walls. A chandelier adds a grace note.

ANTIQUE QUILTS
It's a pleasure to live with the artistry and craftsmanship of these pieces every day. Use them as coverlets, or hang them on the wall.

BARN-INSPIRED PIECES Every farmhouse has (or had) a barn—and furniture with its rustic look is a natural fit.

ELEMENTS OF DOWN-HOME CHARM

Comfortable and inviting without being fussy or fancy—that's the old-fashioned farmhouse aesthetic. Here's how to get it.

FLORAL WALLPAPER
Garden-fresh prints on the wall bring the outside in, all year long.

BOLD PATTERNS
Don't be shy! Chintzes and checks are farmhouse upholstery classics.

A FARM TABLE
Whether it's to use as an island or as the place where your family gathers for dinner, a rustic farm table is the centerpiece of a farmhouse kitchen.

FAMILY HEIRLOOMS
Furniture that has been passed down for a generation or two comes with built-in love.

COLLECTIBLES
Jadeite, milkglass, yellowware—all are perfect for farmhouse display.

BOLD PAINTED PIECES
Gussying up a hand-me-down with bright paint is a thrifty, time-honored move.

WEATHERED FURNITURE
Appreciate the beautiful patina that occurs naturally.

CHAPTER 2

LIVING HISTORY

Some people visit Williamsburg and other enclaves where the past is preserved on vacation—but other folks live with history every day at home. Rustic residences cry out to be complemented with period furnishings, of course, but it goes beyond antique chairs, chests, and textiles. These are homes where vintage appliances look perfectly at ease in the kitchen, and where all the curiosities of the antiques mall—old telephones, farm implements—can be pressed into service as objects of interest. Read on to see the past made perfect in a myriad of individual ways.

The breakfast room in this 1700s Earlton, New York, home had original painted hardwood floors buried under three layers of linoleum tiles. The owners unearthed them, and added reclaimed barnwood paneling and a flea-market table with mismatched chairs.

Settle In

Historical style is often spare, but it offers its own kind of comfort. Seats in front of a roaring fire with portraits of ancestors (not necessarily your own) hung above, or an upholstered window seat-cum-reading nook provide a place to sit and contemplate as long as you like.

In an 1830s New York State farmhouse, a newly commissioned Rumford fireplace is flanked by Windsor chairs from a vintage store in Hudson.

The living room of this 1790s home in Old Chatham, New York, turns a necessity—a radiator—into a delightful window seat with a few John Robshaw throw pillows.

Home, Historic Home

The 1770s home shown here had been victimized by too many remodels-gone-wrong by the time its current owners arrived. They carefully added back a sense of history by coating the walls with two tones of blue-gray plaster (its irregular texture adds old-world romance). Well worth preserving was the home's original millwork—wide-plank hardwood floors and ceiling beams. The result is warm and welcoming.

↓ Patterned area rugs subdivide a large living room into more intimate zones with specific purposes. Quirky arrangements of vintage botanical prints and oil paintings reinforce the collected-over-time vibe.

A narrow, seven-foot-wide back porch seems roomy with vintage wicker and rattan chairs arranged into seating groups. Walls, floors, and ceilings are all painted the same shade of deep blue, which adds to the sense of spaciousness and matches the historical feeling of the home.

Getting Down to Business

Farmhouses were places where people undertook the serious work of preparing and preserving food. So it makes sense that functional items would be placed center stage in the décor. Whether you actually use these items or whether they're more about creating ambience is up to you.

The mudroom sets the tone in this antique farmhouse. Horse tack hangs from a hook, ready to saddle up. Above, a variety of collectibles line the ledge.

A 1932 Magic Chef oven—with six burners and two ovens—holds pride of place in the kitchen of the same home.

Old-Time Kitchen Charm

Kitchens are the undisputed hearts of farmhouses, and putting treasures on display there makes perfect sense because they're easier to grab and use . . . or to just view and enjoy.

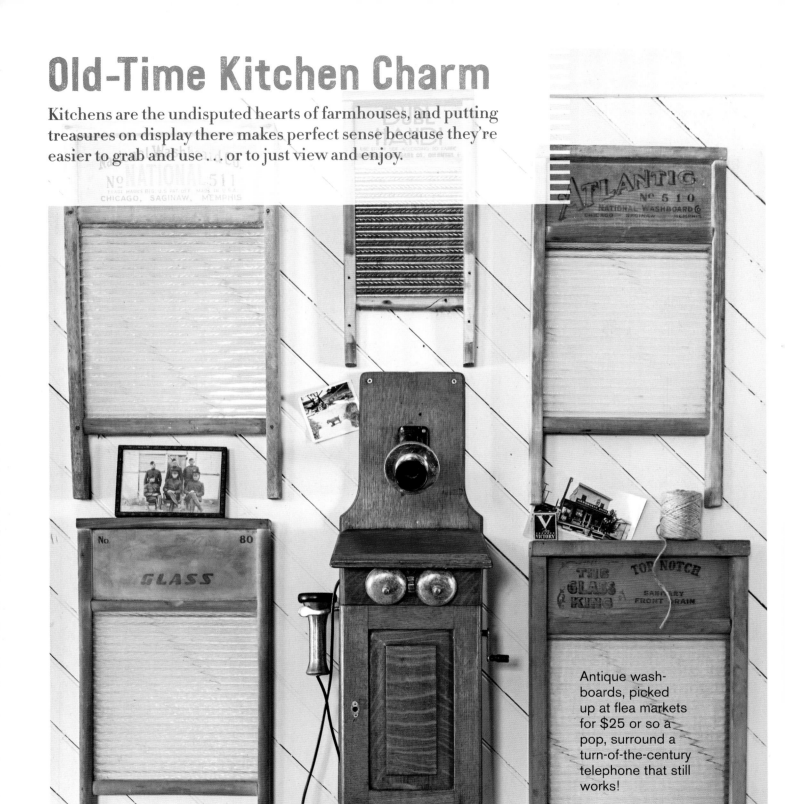

Antique washboards, picked up at flea markets for $25 or so a pop, surround a turn-of-the-century telephone that still works!

SPATTERWARE

GENIUNE 18TH- AND 19TH-CENTURY SPATTERWARE IS A TREASURE BUT LOVELY MODERN VERSIONS ARE EASY TO FIND. SOME OF THE NICEST EXAMPLES ARE MADE BY BENNINGTON POTTERS. IN THE 1970s, THE COMPANY'S FOUNDER, DAVID GILL, PERFECTED A GLAZE-BLOWING TECHNIQUE THAT ALLOWED HIM TO REPLICATE THE SPATTERWARE STYLE FOR LARGE PRODUCTION. IN 2008, PRESIDENT BARACK OBAMA AND HIS FAMILY SELECTED THE COMPANY'S BLUE AGATE SPATTERWARE FOR THEIR WHITE HOUSE RESIDENCE.

New and old flea-market dishware in a hand-built hutch adds a serene, organized, and lovely note.

47

A local carpenter constructed the cabinets, painted black to match the range. The bricks in the floor are from the home's old chimney—and heated radiantly.

Order, Restored

The kitchen in this 1770s New York State home has a hardworking, downstairs-at-Downton-Abbey vibe, with a black La Cornue stove, dark soapstone counters, and a floor of salvaged bricks. The homeowner limited the black cabinetry to lower units in order to install a bank of windows at eye level. The result is a room not only up for major culinary challenges, but homey enough that the family gathers there for every meal.

BRIGHT IDEA: A secondhand brass desk lamp on the cabinet gives the kitchen cozy style.

A Sense of Warmth

Textiles bring a snug feeling to any home—a throw on the couch ready for your afternoon nap, carpeting that softens footsteps and keeps bare feet warm. In a period house, decorating with handwoven blankets and coverlets from times gone by is a graceful way to pay homage to the structure's provenance.

↑ This 1830s farmhouse in New York State is on a remote location amid 75 acres, so window treatments were unnecessary. Instead, textiles were pressed into service in the form of mid-1800s homespun blankets used to cover the ottoman and hardwood floor.

In the master bedroom of the
same home, an 1854 textile is
hung in place of a headboard.
The maker's name and the date
are stitched into the corner.

Just Enough

While old-fashioned can mean over-stuffed, in fact, historical rooms are often spare, with a Shaker-like elegance that comes from having only exactly what you need.

←The kitchen of this 1800s farmhouse steps back in time. It is furnished simply with an oak table and mismatched chairs that are flea-market finds.

→This entry hallway—where a peg rack hung over a rustic bench creates a spot to pull off boots and hang up coats—has few objects yet still brims with character and old-world romance.

Less Is More

The master bedroom and bath in this 1790s Old Chatham, New York, home display a spare aesthetic that feels airy and light. Simply White by Benjamin Moore is used on the walls and highlights the texture of the wide plank paneling.

BRIGHT IDEA: Use antique tables to store towels and toiletries.

←A trifold shaving mirror from Rural Residence in Hudson, New York, and a narrow wire shelf take the place of a medicine cabinet.

An open four-poster bed adds to the sense of space. In contrast, an assortment of family photos hangs above a mid-century armoire.

On the island shelf, a pair of baskets and a vintage galvanized tack box make an attractive spot for stashing unsightly grocery totes and bulky bakeware.

Built for Business

The kitchen on this farm was once a horse stable. Now it is a handsome and hardworking space with reclaimed wood, antique furnishings, and vintage fixtures.

Naturally Curious

Victorians had an insatiable thirst for knowledge about the natural world. It was reflected in décor that brought plants, insects, and animals into the home for closer scrutiny on a daily basis.

↑ Framed vintage butterfly specimens hover above a tufted ticking-stripe armchair in a New York State farmhouse.

← Woodland animal prints are hung on the barn-wood walls of the mudroom in this antique home.

A taxidermied pheasant perches on an 1840s Louis Philippe secretary carved from Cuban mahogany.

HANDWOVEN TEXTILES
Vintage coverlets can be used as throws, rugs, or even upholstery.

RECLAIMED BARN WOOD
Covering the walls with rough-hewn salvaged timbers makes a house feel country again.

ELEMENTS OF HISTORIC STYLE

Here's how to make the past come alive in your home.

ANTIQUE APPLIANCES
A period stove adds authentic character—even if it's not as old as the house.

VINTAGE ART
Whether treasured family portraits or flea-market finds, vintage prints and paintings deliver personality.

SPATTERWARE
This time-honored pattern strikes a historical note with modern graphic appeal.

ORIENTAL AREA RUGS
These carpets define a space with old-world charm.

TAXIDERMY
From stags to pheasants, animals were attractions in early American homes.

BRASS ACCENTS
Brass hardware and lighting—like the secondhand desk lamp shown here—provide warmth.

OLD GLASSWARE
Ball jars, oil lamps, and other antique glass are timeless country accents.

CHAPTER 3

COUNTRY WITH CHARACTER

Not all country style has an eye to the past. Sometimes it's rooted firmly in the present. The wonderful bones of old farmhouses, cabins, and barns are a textured canvas for an eclectic approach that combines antiques and salvaged fixtures with quirky finds and occasional mid-century or modern pieces. The result is a home that's highly personal and as unique to you as your fingerprint.

This "classic" country parlor is charmingly off-kilter. Oversize reproduction shipyard lanterns illuminate in place of expected floor lamps, and a sofa is swapped out for a daybed. A trunk with a weathered patina rounds out the room.

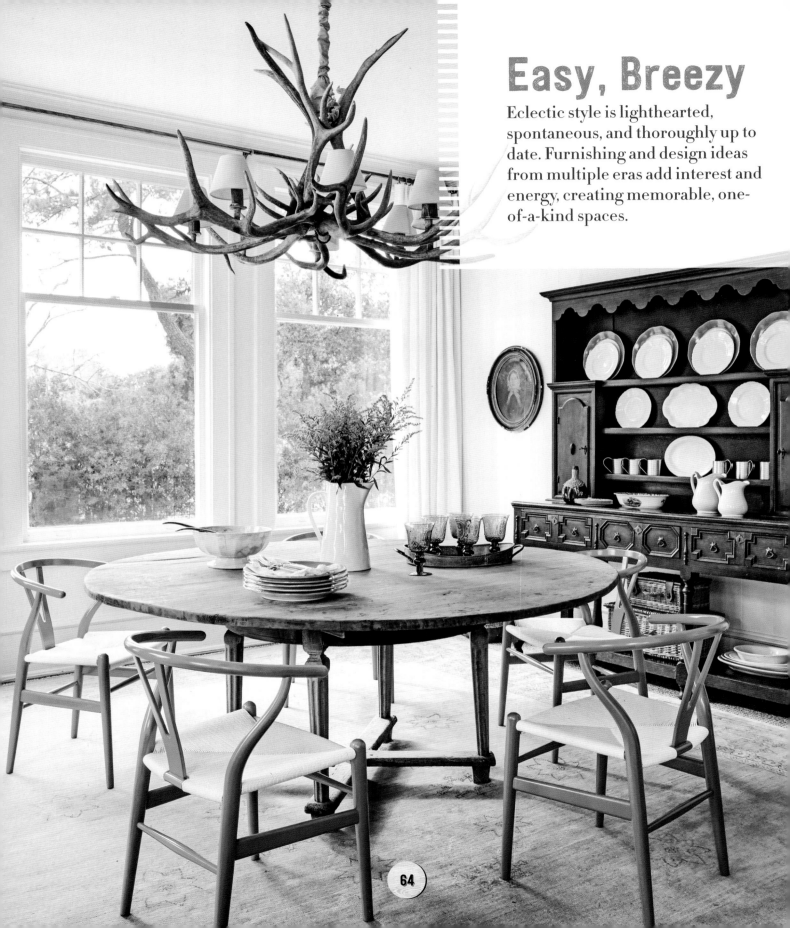

Easy, Breezy

Eclectic style is lighthearted, spontaneous, and thoroughly up to date. Furnishing and design ideas from multiple eras add interest and energy, creating memorable, one-of-a-kind spaces.

← The lush landscape outside inspired this homeowner to fill the dining room with rustic wood and pops of green. Previous residents had left behind the giant antler chandelier. A stripped-down antique round table is surrounded by beech wishbone chairs, lacquered in an apple-green shade for a lively juxtaposition.

→ Trellis wallpaper lining the stair treads adds a contemporary motif among the many weathered finds, such as the collection of straw hats and the oars (one mounted as a handrail!).

Happy-Go-Lucky

Intrinsically optimistic and upbeat, eclectic style is founded on a belief that decorating is closer to play than serious business. A whimsical piece can be just what's needed to make a room—or a nook—into something special.

In this California cabin, West Elm chairs and an Ikea aluminum pendant lamp are set off by adorable curtains stitched from Thomas Paul's dragonfly fabric, which perfectly complements the sylvan views.

Stumbling upon a vintage phone inspired this Tennessee homeowner to turn a closet into a phone booth jam-packed with appeal. A graphic scarlet design on a pillow echoes the arrow on the sign above, and both provide an excellent counterpoint to the old-fashioned beadboard and comfy striped fabrics.

The formal paneling and dramatic chandelier nod to this dining room's former grandeur, but a weather vane found in a Pennsylvania attic and a 1915 Excelsior motorcycle bought from the great-grandson of the original owner unmistakably reflect the tastes of the people who live here now.

Be a Character

It's your home. Why should it look like anyone else's? Have the courage to break the rules!

BRIGHT IDEA: Local accents—like the life preserver in this coastal home—provide color.

This dining table proves to be a showstopper thanks to its massive circa-1880s corbels and bright-blue shutters. Topped with a sheet of glass (cut with smooth, rounded edges), the standout combo anchors the eating area with one-of-a-kind style.

BRIGHT IDEA: On the wall, kitchen tiles rise to the ceiling rather than stopping at backsplash height.

Simple Solutions

Eclectic style is forgiving, and easy upgrades have a big payoff. Perfection isn't the goal here. A personal, lived-in look is.

← The owner of this 19th-century home switched out run-of-the-mill pendant lights with antique versions for instant wow factor. With still-functioning pulleys, these industrial numbers (once used in a billiards hall) make for eye-catching, hardworking task lighting above the island.

→ In this California cabin kitchen, a custom pot rack and spice shelf were built from affordable, preplaned maple—no sanding required. Bright red-latex enamel revived the laminate countertops.

In this woodsy California cabin, a farmhouse-style console table shelters two statement chevron-patterned poufs, which provide extra seating.

BRIGHT IDEA: A ten-foot screen for the room's Panasonic projector is discreetly suspended from the ceiling.

Opposites Attract

Once you free your mind from the idea that a room—or a house—needs to be all one style, the possibilities are endless. New mixes with old, fancy with casual, fine with frayed.

↑ A light fixture from an Ohio barn and a guitar strike country notes in an otherwise formal dining alcove.

→ A mid-century chair, wicker basket, and distressed hutch come from three different backgrounds—but together they work in a perfectly imperfect way.

Worldly Wise

When you're mixing things up, look beyond the U.S.A. Vintage pieces with foreign flair add a well-traveled air to country rooms.

A graphic hotel sign draws attention away from the hardworking heat and air wall unit just above.

THE FRENCH HÔTELS

BRIGHT IDEA: A salmon-hued table and church pew outfitted with feather-down pillows transition to an extra dining space in a pinch.

Pigs are country, whether in France or in this Texas cabin. The Gallic theme is emphasized by a toile-like pillow on the rustic bench below.

Pretty Smart

The freshest looks rely on unexpected pairings that somehow work. Sometimes it's a similar tone that pulls the objects together; other times it's more of a mystery. But when it's successful, the proof is there for all to see.

←A luxuriously long French sofa anchors the room and provides abundant seating. It's covered in durable, affordable paint drop cloths—a workaday note that jibes with the rough-hewn unfinished coffee table.

→A black-hued chowder-house sign and porthole lined with a photo of ocean waves hang happily together above a bar cart because their patina and sophisticated color schemes are in sync.

Farmhouse style—a ticking stripe-upholstered sofa and classics like a pine trunk, rush-seated chair, and spindle table look fresh against bright yellow walls.

On a Deadline?

If you need to furnish a room fast, follow in the footsteps of the *Country Living* editor who created this room in less than two weeks (despite the fact that it looks as if it were assembled over time after countless trips to antiques stores and yard sales). Her secret: internet sources such as Etsy, eBay, and Craigslist. As a bonus, every piece qualifies as a steal.

HOW VALUABLE IS AN ANTIQUE CHEST?

ANTIQUE CHESTS ARE COMMON BECAUSE THERE WERE SO FEW CLOSETS IN 19TH-CENTURY HOMES. MANY OF THEM WERE USED TO STORE BLANKETS. IT IS ALWAYS BETTER TO LEAVE ANY ORIGINAL PAPER OR PAINT ON THE CHEST INTACT, SINCE THAT IS PART OF ITS HISTORY.

In the Mix

Both of these beautiful dining rooms started out with the advantage of the architectural character only an antique farmhouse can provide. But the homeowners went on to prove that noteworthy spaces can be put together on a startlingly tiny budget.

BRIGHT IDEA: A weathered blue window frame now holds a mirror.

Director's chairs from Pier 1 surround a ten-foot-long table constructed of reclaimed barn wood. The owners of this New York State home created the buffet from pine board and $9 trestles from Ikea.

Down-home style and straight-from-the-store don't usually match up. The owner of this Texas farmhouse found the pine dining table on Craigslist for $200, then collected antique bentwood chairs over time. Wicker chairs (one at each end of the table), buffalo check curtains, and a weathered hutch round out the come-as-you-are vibe.

BRIGHT IDEA: A dining-height table was cut down to coffee-table size.

Eclectic Style Is Thrifty

There's no smarter way to stretch your decorating dollars than to embrace a casual, creative, everything-works aesthetic. This beautiful Ashland, Oregon, living room—a product of hand-me-downs and resourceful ideas—is proof of that.

A cast-off sofa re-covered in $7-a-yard canvas, a table discovered unused in a friend's attic, pillows re-covered in fabric from one $60 curtain, and a layered window treatment ($30 shades framed by $19 sailcloth panels) add up to an inviting room with professional polish.

Beauty For A Song

One way to do cheap chic: go with a muted, neutral palette, enlivened by mixing textures and tones. For example, the vignette atop the table (below) incorporates inexpensive wicker-covered jugs, a reasonably priced teapot, and old door knobs. The natural mantel tableaux (right) could be amassed for free by an intrepid beach-goer or "collected" for a few dollars at save-on-crafts.com.

The alabaster lamp was a swap-meet bargain. The homeowner bought it for just $15, rewired it with a kit from a hardware store, and topped it with a Target shade.

A salvage-yard mantel (cost: $250) added instant architectural interest to the living room. The mirror above was assembled by the homeowner, who paid $25 for the vintage plaster-relief frame, then had a beveled mirror cut to fit at a local glass shop for $20.

BRIGHT IDEA: Mismatched armchairs look like a pair when upholstered in the same fabric and painted white.

Vivid Hues

Not only are cheerful colors an instant mood-lifter—they also add interest and character, and are another way to help disparate styles work together.

In this 18th-century Vermont farmhouse, rough-hewn meets bright. An old farm table is classic early-American, but the French armchairs nearby covered in tomato-hued fabric and the yellow mantel take things in an unexpected direction.

87

The damask-like wallpaper in this bathroom was created with a $30 stencil and red paint. The landscape paintings are thrift-shop finds.

VINTAGE ACCENTS
Search out pieces that look as if they have a bit of history behind them.

SALVAGED FIXTURES
Antique (or antique-inspired) lighting instantly transforms a room. There's no faster way to make a cozy statement.

ELEMENTS OF ECLECTIC COUNTRY STYLE

It's a delightful mish-mash of old and new, precious and reclaimed, raw and refined. Here's how to get the look.

GRAPHIC WALLPAPER
There's something unequivocally country about decorating every surface of your home, even the stairs.

VINTAGE SPORTS EQUIPMENT Oars, skis, or tennis rackets add interest hanging on a wall or standing in a corner—especially if they're colorful.

MID-CENTURY MODERN CHAIRS Their bold curves update traditional country antiques.

RUSTIC TABLE Primitive pieces pair well with more refined upholstered sofas and chairs.

WHIMSICAL FINDS If it works because it reflects your personality, your hobbies, or your location, go for it!

TRASH-TURNED-TREASURE Architectural castoffs imbue instant quirky character when used as indoor sculptures.

BOLD CONTEMPORARY PATTERNS A new statement piece adds oomph to a room filled with well-loved vintage furniture.

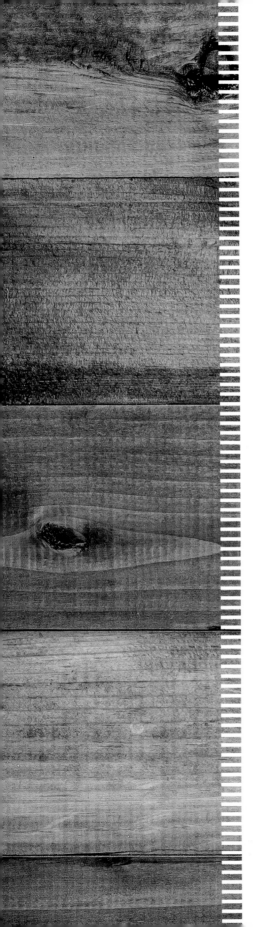

CHAPTER 4

WILD STYLE

Barns, sheds, and other structures that started out as work spaces naturally lend themselves to an unpolished, rough-hewn, rustic style, but so do cabins and some farmhouses. Against a backdrop of weathered wooden walls and floors, giant stone hearths, and exposed ceiling beams, decor such as Hudson's Bay and Navajo blankets, leather upholstery, mounted deer heads, and rich tones of red and green seem right at home. It's a style perfect for a weekend retreat in the mountains or the woods.

Rustic yet refined, this cabin's dining room is anchored by a colorful Navajo rug and punctuated by an antler chandelier. In between, a painted bench and black Windsor chairs pull up to a farm table.

Moments in the Woods

Rustic homes bring elements of the outside in—especially wood! Unpainted, unfinished, and—in some cases—with bark still intact, the surfaces are a constant, cozy reminder of the not-always-friendly environment just beyond the walls.

BRIGHT IDEA: Pinecones and evergreen branches offer an unfussy alternative to a floral centerpiece.

←When the owners of this Vermont cabin decided to expand, they built additions to the original structure, leaving it intact. Now former exterior walls are indoors, as in the dining area, where a 1930s rectangular rag rug pairs with an antique French-Canadian dining table.

→In a contemporary lake house in Vermont, bark-on birch trunks were used to support the library's twelve-foot-long table and built-in bookshelves.

Naturally Warm

These cabin kitchens, one in Tennessee (this page) and one in Vermont (at right), are welcoming and homey. Colorful islands stand out cheerfully amid the dark wood, and stools invite visitors to take a load off and enjoy something wonderful fresh from the oven.

An industrial worktable topped with cut glass is matched by stools also rescued from a factory. A vintage icebox offers hidden storage, while open Douglas-fir shelves hold dishes and cookware.

A 19th-century pine island and Adirondack-style stools do double duty, offering serving and seating options, while also dividing the kitchen from a sitting area in the same great room.

BRIGHT IDEA: Bring outdoor chairs indoors. These are from the 1930s, and were re-covered in plaid Donghia fabric.

Happy Places

Cabins may harken back to a time when life was hard, but they certainly don't need to be grim. In fact, a note of whimsy is all the more welcome in such a resolutely down-to-earth home.

BRIGHT IDEA: Make year-round décor holiday ready by adding fake snow and plastic reindeer or other animals.

←Oversized bright-green shears that once advertised a tailor shop hang above a toy log cabin nestled atop a red-and-white cottage-style chest.

→Candy-striped wallpaper sets the festive stage for a custom-made cherry bed dressed with an antique blanket, shams, and throw pillows.

Cabins and other rough-hewn abodes marry well with furnishings that speak of life's finer things. Beautiful rugs, sophisticated upholstery, and polished furniture complement the structures' rusticity.

Lee Jofa fabric, provide prime seating in the den of this Vermont cabin, rugs—one on the floor, another framed above the fireplace.

The oldest building on Washington's Vashon Island, this cabin boasts an entryway with an oriental rug, a mahogany sideboard, and, occasionally, a curious dairy cow.

99

High Brow

In olden days, cabin dwellers on the frontier passed the evenings playing games, reading, and enjoying the company of friends. Turns out modern-day cabin dwellers aren't so different.

In the library of this Georgia cabin, stately black-and-white buffalo check wing chairs provide a cozy spot for recreation and settling down with a book. The built-in bookshelves are crafted out of tobacco poles and unsanded barn wood.

What better place to spend time with guests than on this Tennessee cabin porch outfitted with a daybed and oriental rugs?

101

Log-Cabin Luxe

In this Michigan cabin, a retired fashion designer and his wife created major drama with rustic mainstays such as twiggy furniture, Hudson's Bay blankets, and matte pottery. Contrast and judicious pops of color are two of the secrets behind the magic.

The dining room's striking drapes were stitched from Hudson's Bay blankets.

White pottery really pops when set on black ledges against a white wall.

Deer antlers hang above a 1930s pine-cabinet dartboard on the four-season porch. This new chair could pass for one of the Old Hickory antiques that came with the home.

←In this 1932 Michigan cabin, the most recent homeowner partitioned a section of the basement to create room for a bath. He constructed the shelf beneath the mirror from fragments of an old dresser.

BRIGHT IDEA: Use hard-wearing Rust-Oleum paint to unify formerly unrelated pieces like the shelf and the flea-market chest below.

American Ingenuity

With their homemade aesthetic, cabins seem to welcome improvisation and clever solutions. Humble and timeworn, these flexible spaces just keep on adapting.

The same homeowner concealed the kitchen's dishwasher with a pine front, which mimics the other cabinetry. He also crafted the window's trompe l'oeil valance—actually a wooden shelf.

105

Fun Home

Cabins don't have to take themselves too seriously. The rustic construction says the opposite of "handle with care." Often weekend or vacation homes, they're meant to be places where a good time is had by all. And their décor can reflect that expectation.

Retro metal signs add a lively, graphic touch to the stairwell of this north Georgia cabin.

In the pantry of this Tennessee cabin, letters spell out just one of many possibilities for the spices displayed on the open shelving.

JAMBALAYA

HOW TO WEATHER WOOD

IF YOU LOVE THE BEEN-AROUND-FOREVER LOOK OF OPEN SHELVING (RIGHT), HERE'S A SECRET: THE WOOD IS BRAND-NEW RED OAK THAT ACQUIRED INSTANT AGE WITH A FEW HOUSEHOLD STAPLES. TO GET THE LOOK: FILL A QUART MASON JAR WITH WHITE VINEGAR AND ADD ONE POUF OF STEEL WOOL. SEAL AND LET SIT FOR AT LEAST 24 HOURS SO THE STEEL WOOL CAN DISSOLVE. NEXT, APPLY A SINGLE LAYER TO THE WOOD (MOST ANY TYPE OF UNFINISHED WOOD WILL DO) USING A PAINTBRUSH. WHEN DRY, ADD A COAT OF WAX (CLEAR BRIWAX) TO PREVENT WATER SPOTTING. NOTE: BECAUSE OF DIFFERING TANNIC ACID LEVELS, SOME WOODS, SUCH AS OAK, WILL STAIN DARKER THAN OTHERS. DILUTE THE SOLUTION WITH WATER IF DESIRED.

Hits of red (including the flag with the cross of St. Patrick to celebrate the owner's Irish heritage) keep the room feeling warm and cohesive.

BRIGHT IDEA: Corrugated metal (rescued from the roof of a falling-down barn) breaks up the large white wall and adds patina.

Country Contemporary

A more appealing, harder-working room is tough to imagine. An Oriental rug and graphic gray gallery wall strike classy, classic notes, while drop-cloth slipcovered furniture is cushy and inviting. The coffee table and chairs add hits of industrial style. It's a rustic, resilient space made for living.

The poplar 1940s headboards are painted with floral detail. Nestled between the beds, an old metal washtub turned upside down works as a nightstand.

BRIGHT IDEA: Declare your pride of place by turning state maps into artwork.

Sleep Tight

Some of the warmest, most welcoming bedrooms have unquestionably rustic roots. At a compound in Kentucky, a chicken coop (opposite) has been transformed into a guest cottage. In a cabin on a New Hampshire lake (above), a sleeping loft is one of the coziest places to bed down.

The sleeping loft's futons wear vintage plaid wool throw pillows and blue-striped coverlets. A chevron runner streaks down the middle of the room.

111

A Shed of Her Own

The ultimate rustic retreat may well be one in your own backyard. Whether it's a place for a solo getaway, parties, or a cottage for guests, all you need is an ordinary shed purchased from Home Depot and a bit of ingenuity.

A loft provides additional sleeping space, and an oversize vintage American flag sets a festive and patriotic tone for backyard get-togethers.

A daybed offers seating and sleeping space inside a twelve-by-sixteen-foot shed.

→ To equip the space for entertaining, add a mini fridge and an assortment of whitewashed wooden crates with pantry and party essentials. A pair of brushed nickel pendant lights strung from the ceiling gives the shed a homey feel.

PAINTED FURNITURE
In a dark wooden cabin, shades of green and red work especially well.

ELEMENTS OF WILD, RUSTIC STYLE

To give your home the look of a frontier cabin or other rough-hewn spaces, start with these ideas.

VINTAGE SIGNS
The graphic punch and bright colors of old business or road signs enliven wooden cabin walls.

HUDSON'S BAY BLANKETS
The classic primary-colored stripes enliven dark cabins and can serve as throws, bedspreads, or even curtains.

ORIENTAL RUGS
These traditional, refined carpets are a beautiful counterpoint to the rough-hewn cabin aesthetic.

WING CHAIRS
This classic style instantly imparts a note of breeding.

TAXIDERMY
Cabins were made for mounted deer heads. Enough said.

ANTLER CHANDELIER
A fixture made of antlers brings the hunting-lodge vibe right into the dining room.

AMERICAN FLAG
An American flag is the only thing possibly more American than a cabin!

CHAPTER 5

COUNTRY FRESH: CLEAN AND MODERN

Old structures look up-to-date when they take on a style that's bright, spare, and light. A neutral palette brought to life with earthy textures and subtle pops of color creates a serene space, and a barn-inspired home's lofty height soars when its interior is painted white. Small spaces in particular benefit from a light touch, which makes the most of limited square feet. Rustic metal sconces and pendant lighting, often farm equipment repurposed from original barns, keep the look down to earth.

In the upstairs hallway of a home near Nashville, a series of five sliding barn doors add to the bucolic vibe. The American flag has 45 stars and dates to around 1896.

Practically Speaking

It might seem counterintuitive to say that white interiors are the perfect match for busy households, but it's true. Washable slipcovers can be bleached, and the crispness of white and pale tones is a natural match for organizing principles like catchall baskets in a foyer.

BRIGHT IDEA: An old chicken crate makes for a coffee table base with rustic appeal.

←In this 1850s
New York
State home,
historical details
like unpainted
exposed beams
are offset by a
Pottery Barn sofa
slipcovered in
washer-friendly
canvas and a
bolster pillow
stitched from a
grain sack.

→The entryway of
this New Canaan,
Connecticut,
farmhouse is
beautifully geared
for everyday
living. Textured
wallpaper serves
as an inviting
backdrop for a
marble-topped
pine console
table. Below, a
barrel corrals
shoes and a
basket holds extra
throw blankets.

Kitchens That Cook!

An emphasis on simple efficiency is the place where modern and country meet—and in no place is that more evident than the kitchen. Counter space and storage are key concerns, and roomy farmhouses and barns offer plenty of room for more than one cook to pitch in.

BRIGHT IDEA: Corner storage (on the wall and at the end of the island) makes smart use of easily overlooked spaces.

A small 1940s farmhouse in the Alberta, Canada, countryside has a clean kitchen crammed with modern ideas. The homeowner used Ikea's online 3-D kitchen planner to make room for a sixteen-square-foot island, and she skipped curtains to brighten the room's look. Minimalist iron-and-glass pendant features cast plenty of light.

In a barn-inspired home outside Nashville, an abundance of moody gray cabinetry, limestone countertops, and stainless steel appliances add luxe elements to a rough-hewn space. To maximize storage, one half of the island contains a series of baskets and bins. The other half has an additional work surface mounted on casters, to roll away when not in use.

121

To the Touch

The owners of this New Canaan, Connecticut, farmhouse chose a neutral, decidedly country base for their décor. Almost every wall in the house is painted the same shade of white, and most of the furniture is covered in white or neutral linen. But it's far from boring, and the reason is texture. Just consider how many different materials are put to use in the photos here!

↓ A woven chair makes a dramatic foyer statement and provides a texture contrast to the plush striped carpeting on the stairs.

BRIGHT IDEA: The living room's bulky radiators couldn't be moved, so the homeowner just built the shelves around it.

⬆ In the living room, wool blankets and fluffy flokati throws in creamy, off-white shades add softness, while rustic wood accents—a round mirror, the three-legged stool—and a stone fireplace ground the space with earthy elements. On the far wall, a ceramics collection adds another texture.

BOARD-AND-BATTEN PANELING

THIS CHARMING WALL TREATMENT (ABOVE) IS ROOTED IN 19TH-CENTURY BARN DESIGN, IN WHICH VERTICAL "BOARDS" WERE LAID OUT SIDE BY SIDE AND "BATTENS" WERE PLACED ABOVE THE SEAMS TO SEAL THE GAPS AND PROVIDE INSULATION.

Hand-pickled pine walls provide a soothing backdrop for a white sofa, antique pine bench, and furry pouf. A photo by Martin Albert mimics the scene outside.

STYLIST ANDRÉ LEON TALLEY

A Zen Zone

It's hard to imagine a more serene retreat than this monochromatic modern take on a Massachusetts cabin. An array of surfaces provide warmth and interest.

→ A shag rug and chunky fringed throw contrast with the den's towering stone fireplace (which was originally outdoors!).

BRIGHT IDEA: Set a tray atop a sturdy pouf, like this wooden one, for a cool coffee table.

Simply Stunning

An 1870s California wine country home was opened up and renovated with creamy white paneling throughout. The result is a clean, modern-with-character backdrop for a home where antiques mix easily with mass-retailer finds, all in almost exclusively neutral shades.

A duo of handsome sofas—one leather, one velvet, both from a catalog retailer—anchors the living room. The different fabrics and shapes give the pairing a much more organic feel than a matched set would have. On the wall, showstopping baskets collected in Europe by the homeowner are hung in an asymmetric configuration. The arrangement brings texture and tonal hues that feel at home amongst the contemporary pieces.

Well Placed

The essence of modern style is edited and organized. There's not a lot of stuff, and what is there knows where it belongs. Shelves and cubbies help keep order. The result is a pleasing sense of life under control, and the assurance that you can find whatever you need exactly when you need it!

← Built-in bookshelves blend seamlessly with this Massachusetts home's hand-pickled pine walls for a streamlined look. The spines of the books continue the light color scheme. A nearby 1970s bentwood rocker softened with a sheepskin beckons browsers to sit and read.

→ In the same home, a floating pine shelf in the entryway offers a spot for bags, shoes, and mail. Steel hooks corral coats, scarves, and more, encouraging order the moment one steps through the door.

A built-in banquette maximizes space and is paired with an antique pine table and school-house chairs. Weathered zinc light fixtures look like antiques but are current offerings.

Spare, but not Bare

A modern look starts at the ground and works its way up. In these rooms, a naked wooden floor (in one case covered with a barely there white area rug) creates a clean, unfussy foundation for simple, functional pieces. The result is a contemporary vibe, even if the furniture is vintage.

A wicker sofa, wooden bench and rug in pale shades keep this sun-filled room serene, while an imposing fig tree adds a splash of green.

Pretty fabric seats and pale-blue paint soften the rug-free wooden floor. A single chair accented in bright blue adds a jolt of color. Upping the warmth factor: a wood-burning stove that provides a strong focal point for the light and airy space.

Hints of Color

Modern doesn't have to mean resolutely neutral. A single tone, used sparingly, can enliven a room, adding cheer and appeal. Sea-inspired shades of blue and green work especially well with white and wood, as demonstrated in the pretty rooms shown here.

↑ An antique barn door track gets a second life as a picture rail above the tufted burlap headboard. A folded blue coverlet at the foot of the bed and a blue pillow bring color to the room.

→ A canopy, made of windowpane plaid fabric panels hung from a frame of simple crown molding, fills this home's master bedroom with softly colorful texture.

↑ A stunning collection of colorful glass demijohn bottles makes a statement on the dining area's built-in shelves. The black iron chandelier—a flea-market find—is decked out in alternating black and white shades made by the homeowner.

WHAT IS A DEMIJOHN BOTTLE?

THESE GLASS VESSELS, ALSO REFERRED TO AS "CARBOYS," ARE CHARACTERIZED BY THEIR ROUND SHAPES AND SHORT, NARROW NECKS. USED FOR STORING LIQUIDS AND FERMENTING SPIRITS, THEY WERE ORIGINALLY COVERED IN WICKER, WHICH PROTECTED THE GLASS. THE ORIGIN OF THE WORD "DEMIJOHN" IS UNCLEAR: IT MAY DERIVE FROM "DAMGHAN," A PERSIAN TOWN KNOWN FOR GLASSMAKING, OR FROM "DAME JEANNE," AS SUCH BOTTLES ARE REFERRED TO IN FRANCE.

Cool but Cozy

Clean, modern interiors can have all the warmth you'd expect to find in a snug farmhouse. In this home, the natural treatment of the wood creates a smooth, soft-looking, touch-me texture and makes the house feel like part of the great outdoors, rather than a retreat from it.

This inviting guest bed is dressed with a pin-tucked cotton blanket, a tasseled throw, and a bleached canvas duvet. Swaths of linen bring subtle interest to an upholstered headboard, and sliding barn doors free up floor space in the small bedroom.

A stone wall brings an earthy note to the kitchen, where elm slabs cover the island and soft felt cushions top the stools.

BRIGHT IDEA: A simple steel pipe strung with S hooks keeps pans, trivets, and utensils in handy reach.

135

In the master bedroom of this 1940s Canadian farmhouse, a black metal bed with an airy headboard and footboard dominates the room.

This beat-up spring green piece was previously an artist's easel and before that, a handyman's workbench. Now serving as a bar in an alcove off a kitchen, it anchors the space beautifully.

Star Quality

Clean, modern white backgrounds make room for furniture to take on a sculptural quality. Look for pieces with standout style, whether weathered or contemporary.

The zinc and black leather barstools add some edge to a clean, white kitchen. They were modified by a local metal shop to swivel, and create a casual, open feel between the kitchen and the adjoining living room.

Soaring Heights

The 25-foot ceilings in this barn-inspired Tennessee home are emphasized even further by a towering fieldstone fireplace and poplar paneling in varying widths hung vertically and painted a creamy white.

Open and spacious, the sitting room features a modern mix of contemporary oversized wingbacks, an unusual antler chair, and a traditional leather sofa.

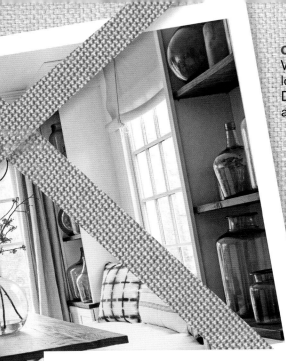

COLORFUL COLLECTIONS
When you find something you love, why not go overboard? Display your finds on shelves and turn walls into sculpture.

SLIPCOVERED FURNITURE
Whether on sofas or chairs, these coverings merge style with practicality.

WOODEN ACCENTS
Little wooden stools and benches provide homespun details and lots of spots to sit.

ELEMENTS OF CLEAN AND MODERN COUNTRY STYLE

Simple rustic touches give a cabin, barn, or farmhouse a fresh, contemporary look.

WOVEN SEATING
Furniture made of sea grass, wicker, or rattan complements any look and lasts a lifetime.

PLANTS Lush leaves, whether real or silk, add welcome vibrancy to modern, neutral homes.

BARN DOORS
Sliding doors add country appeal and are also a great space-saver.

BASKETS
They're the perfect place to stash clutter in a streamlined home.

COFFEE TABLE
Furniture made from "use what you've got" pieces like an old chicken crate brings a rustic counterpoint to a modern room.

SHELVES AND CUBBIES
A modern look is organized. Keep it clean with lots of storage.

NUBBY FIBERS
Add texture with soft rugs and throws.

CHAPTER 6

NEW MADE OLD

Even suburban ranch houses and new constructions can have a been-around-forever feeling when homeowners look to farmhouses, barns, and cabins for their inspiration. While new homes are sometimes designed using reclaimed wood and vintage fixtures that make them virtually indistinguishable from an antique, any home can possess a bit of rustic charm. Ceiling beams, farmhouse sinks, wood paneling, and barn-style lighting are just a few of the classic, character-building moves you can make no matter what kind of house you call home.

This newly built Jackson, Wyoming, retreat is a modern log cabin with design ideas that make roughing it downright luxurious.

A Light Touch

While a traditional log cabin can easily read masculine, heavy, and dark, the owners of this new Jackson, Wyoming, log home wanted a cozy residence with a feminine feeling. One strategy: using colorful floor coverings to add warmth throughout—even in the kitchen!

↑ A plush coffee table in pale blue makes this a living room where ladies and gentlemen can feel at home. The crimson armchairs and pale blue shade combine for a sophisticated pairing.

→ Afraid that too much wood might be stifling, the homeowners chose to paint the kitchen cabinets a warm gray. The result is an airy contrast to the paneling in surrounding rooms.

Frontier Fancy

The walls may be rough in a new (or old) log cabin, but that doesn't mean the living has to be, at all. In this home, the guest bedroom is decorated against type with a chinoiserie chest and beautifully made-up beds.

Because the "bird suite" is long and narrow, the homeowners chose to forego a king-sized bed and instead opted for two queen-sized iron beds to fill the space.

Sleeping Quarters

The owners of this new home knew they wanted to play frequent host to family and friends, so they built accordingly. Inspired by old-fashioned cabin bunk rooms, they constructed six queen-sized bunks instead of the traditional twin. The space also has two twin beds, so it sleeps fourteen altogether!

Each sleeping nook features a hollowed-out alcove with its own outlet for recharging mobile devices and a sconce for late-night reading. Handy drawers are built in below the bunks.

In the home's master bedroom, a whimsical bird bed is outfitted with a Pendleton throw in an unexpectedly subdued shade and paired with a cream matelassé.

149

Reclaimed Rancher

A 1970s ranch house near Atlanta is given a new-old facelift with a reconfigured layout to create wide-open spaces, cohesive architectural details, and oak hardwood flooring throughout.

BRIGHT IDEA: Mix lighting–like the statement-making lantern, picture-light sconces, vintage floor lamp, and striped tabletop one–to make a room even more inviting.

←The library now anchors one end of a long room with a kitchen on the other end and a farmhouse table for eating in the middle (not shown). Vertical spruce-plank clads the walls and makes the space feel like the inside of an old barn that's been updated with a fresh coat of white paint.

→Vertical painted stripes give the hallway decorative oomph on a budget and make the eight-foot ceilings (typical for a rancher) seem taller. A primitive workbench and demijohn jar provide color and texture.

Character Study

A few strategic additions can take a house from suburban cookie cutter to one-of-a-kind personality. In this Atlanta rancher, a reclaimed beam on the kitchen ceiling and a rough-hewn mantel grafted onto the living room's stone fireplace (not shown) add individuality. A black fireclay sink in the kitchen and an unexpectedly ornate mirror in the powder room carry out the country theme.

A black fireclay sink is dressed up with a skirt made from fabric the homeowner admits was a splurge. The oriental rug is a favorite spot for the family's pooch.

←Four wood-and-metal bar stools (found at three different T. J. Maxx locations) and picture lights that illuminate both an art collection and countertop work space guarantee that this kitchen is different from any other on the street.

→In the powder room, graphic plaid wallpaper plays background to the fancy carved wooden mirror. Silhouettes complete the old-fashioned vibe.

If You Build It...

Searching for a country house in Litchfield County, Connecticut, a couple found property they loved with a house that was more rundown than rustic. So they rebuilt, using reclaimed materials for character, but also avoiding typical undesirable qualities of older homes: e.g., small, boxy rooms; little windows; and a tiny kitchen. The result is the best of both worlds, complete with a small replica barn connected to the main house by an enclosed breezeway. With reclaimed wood timbers and a lofted ceiling, it looks as inviting as the real thing.

The house's barn is the family's go-to gathering spot, and thanks to modern trappings like radiant heat and durable engineered wood floors, it's warm and cozy.

Stake Your (Re)Claim

Thanks to its owner's passion for one-of-a-kind found items, this Arizona ranch house is filled with statement-making pieces that give rooms instant patina.

A farm sink is transformed into a stylish wash station with new brass faucets and a gold-framed mirror.

A giant pocket door, salvaged from an old warehouse and trimmed with a map pennant banner, establishes the dining room's layered-over-time vibe, making the secondhand table, mismatched seating, and garage-sale rug look collected, not hodge-podge.

BRIGHT IDEA: Vintage science lab charts become cool wall art!

Three mismatched vintage bed frames coexist happily in a boys' bedroom when dressed with matching bedding. A set of old nautical light fixtures also helps create a cohesive look.

A 1920s claw-foot tub with added polished brass fixtures inspires this bathroom's old-meets-new mix. Black porcelain floor tile, laid in a herringbone pattern, adds a bit of edge, while a chippy green chair, an antique Moroccan lantern, and a storage cabinet salvaged from an aircraft carrier offset the sleek surfaces.

Good Old Things

Antiques can give a modern home a been-there-forever feeling. When they're mixed with bold colors and prints in a 1970s-era house, they fit right in.

159

Country Cool

In a newly built Newport Beach, California, farmhouse, clean meets rustic for a sunny, come-as-you-are feeling.

← A barn-wood accent wall paired with old stadium seating and abstract artwork sets the tone in the home's entryway.

The living room was designed with rural style to the hilt: a steep-pitched ceiling, paneled walls, wood floors, and an influx of natural light. A wooden filly—nearly six feet wide—makes a modern, graphic statement.

Back to the Barn

These new farmhouse kitchens trace their inspiration right out to the stable.

An X-brace supports and adds warmth to this marble-topped island. Other wood embellishments: a band of reclaimed boards around the sleek range hood and ceiling beams.

GROCERY

In this new Texas kitchen, two panels reminiscent of barn doors hide the pantry.

163

A custom-built ladder accesses the sleeping loft tucked above the dining area in the home's open main room.

The Cabin, Reimagined

This new 600-square-foot cabin in Idaho was built with a modern eye. Floor-to-ceiling windows frame mountains in every direction, and squared, rather than rounded, logs create clean-lined walls.

A vintage claw-foot tub graces the bedroom, along with a warm sheepskin rug. A Pendleton blanket and shams dress the bed.

BOTANICAL MOTIFS
Whether in frames or on pillows, green leaves have a way of freshening things up.

TOUCHES OF BLACK
The shade grounds a room and harkens back to old farm equipment.

ELEMENTS OF NEW-MADE-OLD STYLE

To give your new home a been-there-for-years look, start here.

PLANKED WALLS
Run the boards vertically to make a new home's low ceilings look higher.

TIMELESS UPHOLSTERY
For big-ticket items, stick with classic forms and fabrics.

RATTAN PENDANT
Search for pieces that look like they could have had a past life.

X-BRACE DESIGNS
This barn motif can be used on everything from a kitchen island to planters.

REPURPOSED SEATING
Both storied and sturdy, old stadium seats are perfect for a house with kids.

GRAPHIC RUGS
A patterned flat-weave style is made for hiding dirt.

Photo Credits

Index